Contents

INTRODUCTION

With numerous CBD health benefits for dogs,

many pet parents are purchasing CBD dog treats

for their furry best friends. Although they're

available online and in stores, nothing is as much

fun as making them together with your pooch at

home.

Getting to choose which natural ingredients and

flavors to use from like kale-carrot, blueberry-

cranberry, pumpkin harvest flavor or peanut

butter crunch make bakingCBD dog treats at

home a fun experience for all.

You can also opt to use natural, healthy

ingredients to ensure natural macro and micronutrients with no synthetic dyes or preservatives keeping your dog healthy all the way!

That said, it's important to note that CBD oil measurements will vary according to your dog's weight and health. CBD edibles for pets make life much easier, and are fun to bake.

Besides what's better than safe, natural, vegan, and non-GMO baked dog treats for your furry best friend? Keep reading to find out more aboutCBD treats for pets, how to use them, and why they are so popular today?

Pet parents all share an incredible bond, and most of us will do whatever it takes to make our pets feel better. Today, we see CBD as a natural supplement dominating the US's pet and human market in sales. With CBD for pets being legal in the US if it contains less than 0.3 % THC, we all must know as much as possible as to how to use cannabidiol pet products most safely and effectively possible.

The take with pet CBD is that substantial research to investigate the veterinary benefits for pets of cannabidiol is ongoing, with health benefits looking incredibly promising. Today, we're noticing that CBD for pets in the form of hemp-based supplements has become a trending choice. This is because there are very few adverse effects from a high-quality full-spectrum hemp oil.

Research has demonstrated how cannabinoid receptors interact with the endocannabinoids and phytocannabinoids and how CBD may help reduce seizure disorders, chronic neuropathic pain, cancer, and anxiousness, insomnia, and more. In this blog, we'll examine what CBD is and what it can do for your pet? Also, whether CBD is safe for pets?

CBD OIL FOR DOG

Pet parents all share an incredible bond, and most of us will do whatever it takes to make our pets feel better. Today, we see CBD as a natural supplement dominating the US's pet and human market in sales. With CBD for pets being legal in the US if it contains less than 0.3 % THC, we all must know as much as possible as to how to use cannabidiol pet products most safely and effectively possible.

The take with pet CBD is that substantial research to investigate the veterinary benefits for pets of cannabidiol is ongoing, with health benefits looking incredibly promising. Today, we're noticing that CBD for pets in the form of hemp-based supplements has become a trending choice. This is because there are very few adverse effects from a high-quality full-spectrum hemp oil.

Research has demonstrated how cannabinoid receptors interact with the endocannabinoids and phytocannabinoids and how CBD may help reduce seizure disorders, chronic neuropathic pain, cancer, and anxiousness, insomnia, and more. In this blog, we'll examine what CBD is and what it can do for your pet? Also, whether CBD is safe for pets?

WHAT IS CBD?

CBD contains Omega-3 fatty acids that helps to fight inflammation. A recent 2017 STUDY demonstrates that the researchers "found an enzymatic pathway that converts omega-3-derived endocannabinoids into more potent anti-inflammatory molecules that predominantly bind to the receptors found in the immune system." This finding shows how omega-3 fatty acids can produce some of the same medicinal qualities as marijuana, but without a psychotropic effect, via Science Daily.

HERE'S THE DEAL:

Reliable, high-quality CBD brands have numerous health benefits. This is because CBD may help dogs and cats with:

- Inflammatory bowel disease

- Side effects of chemotherapy and radiation

- Chronic pain

- Anxiety

- Seizures and tremors

- Cardiac health

- Autoimmune diseases

- Cancer

- General aches and pain

- Arthritis

- Fear

- Skin irritations

- Skin tumors

Over the past couple of years, veterinarians and pet parents have discovered via research the benefits of cannabidiol to treat numerous health conditions in pets. Today, dogs suffering from an array of medical conditions like seizures, pain, inflammation, cancer, arthritis, and digestive issues have found relief with the use of cannabidiol as a natural supplement.

Cannabidiol offers numerous antioxidant properties that may prevent cancer, treat tumors, manage pain, reduce the side effects of chemo and radiation, and more. That said, it's necessary to choose the right form of administration, capsules, tinctures, edibles, patches, and so forth, to get the best bioavailability for a specific health issue.

Consulting with your dog's veterinarian allows for an accurate CBD brand supplement choice to help with a specific health condition. You'll also be able to discuss dosage and efficacy for your dog or cat's specific health condition.

CBD oil is also packed with important minerals such as iron, zinc, and magnesium, all beneficial for human and pet health. Zinc is important for a good coat and skin in pets.

CBD also yields elastin and collagen that results in a glossy coat. It is brimming with antioxidants and yields vitamins A, E, and C, which fight against free-radicals from pollution.

Cannabidiol works together with the endocannabinoid system (ECS) in both pets and humans and allows for homeostasis. All pets have an endocannabinoid system with neurotransmitters in the endocannabinoid system involved in physiological processes like pain sensation, appetite, mood, and memory.

That said, the endocannabinoid system is similar in all animals, but with differences between species. A dog's endocannabinoid system is different in that dogs have a higher concentration of endocannabinoid receptors in their brainstem and cerebellum than any other species do. These structures control breathing, heart rate, and muscle coordination.

HEMP CBD PET PRODUCTS

When choosing a CBD pet product made from hemp, it's best to opt for high-quality, safe, and effective pet products. It's important to research companies and manufacturing methods before purchasing a product. You'll need to check for complete and accurate labeling to ensure that you have less than 0.3% THC.

You should always begin at the lowest dose and then slowly work up to the as-needed dosing. If you do this, you'll limit the chances of adverse reactions. When using pet cannabidiol products, you should first consult with your veterinarian for a complete diagnosis and to discuss how CBD may be beneficial for your pet. Here's the take with CBD dosing:

• Start with the lowest dosing to prevent adverse reactions, if any.

• Use only pet CBD products with no THC

• Your vet may recommend a specific dosage, which may differ for each pet and each condition.

• The calculated dose should be divided for twice-daily dosing.

• Doses up to 5 mg/kg/day have been recommended for serious seizure cases.

• Follow the biphasic dosing curve when using CBD on pets.

• To make things less complicated, if you're having difficulties finding the right dose for your cat and for some reason are unable to weigh him or her, visit your veterinarian to get his or her correct weight.

A CBD dosage is based on your cat's or dog's weight, so you will need to convert your pet's weight from pounds to kilograms. You can do this by dividing the weight in pounds by 2.2 = 5 kg.

Multiply the mg's in the dose to the number of

kg in weight. If the dose is 0.2 mg/kg, you would

have to multiply 5 kg by 0.2 = 1mg.

CBD OIL FOR CATS

Cannabidiol oil, also known as CBD oil, comes in a

wide array of options for cats like CBD oil

tinctures, treats, capsules, lotions, and can be

taken orally or applied topically to the skin. CBD

products can be applied directly to skin irritations

or hot spots in cats.

Nowadays, cat treats, and cat CBD tinctures are

fast becoming a popular option since cat parents

realize that CBD oil for cats is safe and has very

few side effects. That said, always opt for THC-free CBD cat products, and triple check the potency of all tinctures since they will all vary according to the brand.

DERMATITIS IN CATS & DOGS

CBD tinctures, capsules, topicals, and treats are useful for treating chronic and mild skin conditions in cats. Dermatitis is caused by skin inflammation that may result from allergens, trauma, bacterial, viral, parasitic, or fungal infections, external irritants, burns, and infection. As your pet ages, he may be afflicted with allergies, skin disorders, itchiness, and chronic pain. CBD may be beneficial in managing your furry friend's discomfort, allowing him relief from

inflammation and chronic pain.

CBD AS A SUPERFOOD

CBD is regarded as both a superfood and a

supplement with numerous health benefits

gained by its minerals like iron, zinc, magnesium,

antioxidants, vitamins A, E, and C, which protects

from free-radicals resulting from everyday

pollution.

CBD offers all 21 amino acids, which are the

building blocks of protein. CBD also contains

phytocannabinoids, terpenes, and fatty acids,

which all help with stress relief.

CBD has been proven to help reduce cell damage that occurs from free radicals. That said, cannabidiol oil (CBD) can help dogs with skin allergies, inflammation, itchy skin and promote a healthy coat and skin in dogs. "Cannabidiol, THC, and BHT all prevented dihydroergotamine oxidation in a similar, concentration-dependent manner indicating cannabinoids to be comparable to BHT in antioxidant potency," NCBI.

The study adds that "The antioxidative properties of cannabinoids suggest a therapeutic use as neuroprotective agents, and the particular properties of cannabidiol make it a good candidate for such development.

Although cannabidiol was similar in neuroprotective capacity to BHT, cannabidiol has no known tumor-promoting effects. The lack of psychoactivity associated with cannabidiol allows it to be administered in higher doses than would be possible with psychotropic cannabinoids such as THC."

CBD AS AN ANTI-INFLAMMATORY

CBD for pets may be beneficial for its healing benefits for dogs with inflammation. RESEARCH proves that "Cannabinoids are a group of compounds that mediate their effects through cannabinoid receptors.

"Cannabinoids have exhibited the significant potential to be used as novel anti-inflammatory agents, and specific targeting of CB2 receptors holds the promise of mediating immunosuppressive effects without exerting psychotropic side effects."

A recent 2018 study on CBD and canine arthritis at Cornell University's College of Veterinary Medicine by Dr. Joe Wakshlag tested to see whether pain from osteoarthritis and multi-joint pain could be eliminated CBD oil.

The CBD oil was made from industrial hemp or placebo hemp, and dogs received it every 12 hours for 4 weeks. Cornell worked together with ElleVet Sciences that created soft CBD ElleVet

Mobility chews, which are hemp-based. The chews also contained chondroitin and glucosamine, two natural compounds that help with movement in arthritic dogs.

IS IT SAFE?

Your first question will be, whether it's safe for pets?

When purchasing any cannabidiol pet product, you'll need to ensure that it's made specifically for pets. Full-spectrum hemp oil pet products may be beneficial for anxiety and arthritic pain, as well as other health conditions and your vet may combine both conventional pet meds with a CBD pet product.

When exploring CBD pet products, the most important question is if a product uses an isolate or a full-spectrum oil, which is the most potent and comes from the entire plant. Here's the deal with possible side effects:

• May interact with certain pet meds

• Lowers blood pressure

• Lethargy

• Possible allergic reaction

• Possible lethargy

EXTRACTION METHOD

Extraction of the oil occurs via a carbon dioxide process called CO2 extraction, which entails using pressurized carbon dioxide to extract the CBD from the entire plant. CO2 functions as a solvent when reaching extreme temperatures, yet because it is under boiling point, it's cold. It is processed to create oil from the plant. It is also a clean and environmentally friendly process.

Pet owners should examine all the premium hemp oil extract products to see if they have CBD on the packaging. Due to certain industry requirements, numerous pet products with CBD will only be labeled premium hemp oil extract products.

We all may have become confused with so many CBD products out there on the market! Numerous pet specialty stores have included newsletters and handouts for pet parents to update information on treats and edibles, as well as CBD oils for pets.

Companies like Animal Nutritional Products have based their CBD product line on dealing with serious health issues in dogs like osteoarthritis, anxiety, and urinary tract disease. Here's the take when purchasing:

• Hemp CBD should be 100% food grade.

• Should be made using CO2 extraction

• No solvents like butane

• Full-spectrum lab testing by a third party for

purity and potency

• Lab certificates available for pet owners to

examine before a purchase

• Pesticide and herbicide free

• Made with non-GMO hemp

Consumers are advised to ask whether their CBD

product of choice is a full-spectrum oil or if it

uses an isolate. Also, if the hemp used is from

locally grown USA hemp? European sourced

hemp may have originated from China and ended

up being processed in Europe. That said, hemp

from China is not of as high quality and purity

and may contain bio-contaminants and heavy metals.

SIMPLE TIPS

All pet CBD product potencies are different, so you will have to know the CBD pet product's concentration by understanding how many "mgs" of CBD is in each milliliter of oil? (ml)

Consult with your veterinarian or a CBD cat product expert if you're not 100% sure about dosing.

• Fully panel tested by a third party with a certificate of inspection.

• Varying doses for cats of all sizes

- Ingredients include natural broad-spectrum CBD with DHA, essential oils, and hemp oil.

- Made with natural cannabidiol oil that is organic & vegan

- Oral syringe provided for easier oral administering

- Dosing chart included for safety (call your vet if you don't understand the dosing chart)

- Effective in helping with anxiousness, stressful situations like travel, storms, trips to the vet, & car rides, which most cats dislike

- High-quality CBD cat products have added ingredients for optimal cat health.

• Works fast and may be used together with veterinary-approved pharmaceuticals

• Cost-effective

• Organic and natural with no contaminants like glysophate

• Works with seizures, joint pain, skin allergies, itchy skin, and more

• Veterinarian recommended

• Made especially for cats, an added plus since dosage and efficacy are cat friendly.

• Popular tuna or chicken flavor that cats love

• Non-GMO using C02 extraction for purer quality

• Packed with Omega 3,6,9 for skin, coat, brain health, and anti-inflammatory purposes.

• Easy-to-administer to cats with a dropper

• Contains a high-quality hemp seed oil

• Added vitamins, omega's, terpenoids, flavonoids, and phytochemicals for optimal benefits in cats.

WORK WITH YOUR VETERINARIAN

It's too bad that so many of us grew up with a social stigma attached to THC, marijuana and the like for several reasons that relate to both CBD oil for dogs and CBD oil for cats. First, marijuana, THC and the like have nothing to do with CBD oil and this type of treatment for the conditions we mentioned above. Secondly, this perceived stigma and faulty identification can lead to too many people hesitating to talk about this approach with their veterinarians. That may lead some dogs and cats to suffer needlessly or to be given prescription medications that can in some cases inflict their own types of damage.

Therefore, if you're thinking of using CBD oil for dogs or CBD oil for cats, don't hesitate to talk to your veterinarian. He or she will be receptive to what you're asking about regardless of his or her opinion of this approach. It's legal, it's legitimate and it's worth the modicum of effort required to explore its possibilities. Not to mention, your veterinarian can help you identify the right reasons for treatment, the right products to put to use and with other variables that will likely arise as you move forward. CBD oil for dogs and CBD oil for cats can work wonders, but it's always better to do things like this with medical oversight.

CBD DOG TREATS

CBD is a non-psychotropic phytocannabinoid that offers both therapeutic and medicinal purposes for humans and pets. It is also natural, safe, and is derived from hemp and cannabis. Most CBD dog treats will useCBD from hemp. That said,

there is no "high" and your furry best friend will

not consume THC or tetrahydrocannabinol,

resulting in psychoactive effects with your dog

getting "high".

Cannabidiol dog treats help dogs relax and

become pain –free. The pet industry has watched

the rising popularity of CBD products throughout

2019, and have recognized the effectiveness of

hemp oil to help with chronic pain, anxiety and

other ailments in pets.

Full-spectrum CBD tinctures offer specific

terpenes and active ingredients to address health

issues, including pain and anxiety in pets. Today,

alternate health and wellness options for pets via

natural supplements or nutraceuticals are becoming popular household items because they don't have the side effects of pharmaceuticals. Using natural CBD supplements for pets that utilize nano-sized microemulsion for optimal bioavailability helps to keep your pets healthy and free from pain and suffering.

Your holistic veterinarian will be able to offer you complete guidance on the correct and safe dosage of any CBD pet tinctures. Hemp pet products are natural, safe, and have the potential to help with pain, insomnia, anxiety, and plenty of other health issues in both cats and dogs.

Understanding the importance of transparency in all CBD brands is important when choosing a CBD hemp oil product for your pet. That said, consult with your veterinarian before choosing a CBD pet product and adding it to your pet's regime.

HOW TO USE CBD OIL WHEN BAKING CBD DOG TREATS?

The potency of CBD oils both in capsule form and those in bottles with droppers are much more potent and are sometimes more difficult to administer to dogs that are fussy eaters, or that don't enjoy oral applications. Baking dog treats with hemp oil helps to allow for a relaxed environment where you get to choose your dog's favorite ingredients while baking CBD dog treats.

A few product lines contain phytocannabinoids, terpenes and fatty acids which support a huge range of ailments like phobias, joint pain, inflammation, digestive issues, mobility, seizures, and anxiety. Before using any ingredients for baking, make sure that your dog is not allergic to any of them. Dogsgetfood allergies similar to humans, so it's necessary to look out for certain symptoms that may indicate a food allergy.

Understanding which CBD oil brand to choose from when baking CBD dog treats for your pooch makes things a lot safer and easier. Here's how what you need to know before baking CBD dog treats for your furry best friend:

• Use organic, non-GMO ingredients

• Use all-natural ingredients

• Refrain from using preservatives or synthetic dyes

• Understand what ingredients are safe and which should not be used

• Try to use vegan ingredients

• Calming herbs like chamomile can be added

• Glucosamine and other supplements can be included (consult with your veterinarian)

WHAT YOU NEED TO KNOW

When cooking or baking with CBD, you'll need to keep the following in mind:

• The boiling point for CBD should never be more than 356°F, otherwise, the active constituents will begin to evaporate.

• A good temperature for cooking with CBD should stay between 320°F to 356°F only.

• CBD oil should be infused into fat before cooking with it. This can be either butter, coconut oil, or cooking oil.

• A low heat should be used when blending in the CBD hemp oil and the fat.

• The blended oils should be kept in a dark cupboard away from sunlight for optimal efficacy.

• CBD completely degrades at 329 degrees

Fahrenheit and begins breaking down before

that.

• Flavored CBD oils need to be used with

corresponding ingredients for the best taste

CBD OIL DOG TREAT BENEFITS

CBD offers a wide range of health benefits. That

said, some of these potential benefits include

anxiety relief and pain relief. When taking

cannabidiol oil alone, it may not taste ideal, and

most dogs tend not to enjoy the taste. When

adding cannabidiol oil into a variety of tasty and

healthy dog treats, you'll allow for your pooch to

enjoy them without trying to force him to consume the oil by itself via a tincture.

To get around any confusing issues and conflicting information, always consult with your holistic veterinarian for the best advice before choosing a CBD product for your pooch! Be sure to scan the reviews, and to always opt for the highest-quality, natural CBD product for your pooch! This applies even when you're baking CBD dog treats for your pets. Using high-quality cannabidiol oil when cooking is important. Here are some benefits:

• Pain reliever

• May help with canine depression

- May provide relief from cancer side effects like chemotherapy and radiation

- Promotes skin health by preventing sebaceous gland cells from secreting too much sebum

- May provide benefits dogs with neurological disorders

- Helps decrease inflammation in pets

- May help prevent cognitive decline

- May be beneficial for cardiac health

- CBD may be beneficial in preventing tumor growth

- CBD helps with diabetes prevention by reducing diabetes up to 56% and reducing associated inflammation in diabetic pets.

- Digestive issues

- Blood disorders

- Fights off free radicals and may prevent the

development of cancer

That said, there still needs to be more research

done on the benefits of CBD as an effective

treatment for the above-mentioned health

conditions. Consult with your holistic

veterinarian for advice.

CBD FOOD FOR DOG RECIPES

Sheet-Style CBD Dog Treats

Our first CBD dog treat recipe is likely the most accessible to anyone reading at home. That's because this recipe requires mostly things you already have at home!

Ingredients

• 2 ounces Broad Spectrum CBD Oil (unflavored)

• 1 cup Flour (unbleached, gluten-free)

• 1 cup Oatmeal

• 2 Eggs

• Water (as needed)

Directions

• Preheat your oven to 350°F.

• Grease a small to medium-sized baking sheet.

• In a medium bowl, beat your eggs and flour until mixed; add oatmeal and broad-spectrum CBD oil.

• Add water until your desired thickness is achieved. The mixture should be thick but not overly viscous, similar to pancake batter.

• Smooth the batter evenly atop the baking sheet.

• Bake for 8 minutes.

• Let sit 5 minutes after cooking; cut treats into doggy bite-sized pieces (cookie-cutter optional).

Dogs love a good biscuit. Why not infuse them with CBD oil? These treats for dogs are a little more advanced than sheet-style dog treats but make a great, pet-friendly quarantine cooking project! What will you need to get started?

Ingredients

• 2 ounces Broad Spectrum CBD Oil (unflavored or bacon-flavored)

• 2-½ cups Flour (unbleached, gluten-free)

• ½ cup Oatmeal

• ½ cup Powdered Milk

- ½ cup Creamy Peanut Butter

- 1 Extra-Large Egg

- Egg Wash (1 egg beaten with 1 tablespoon

water)

- Water (as needed)

Direction

- Preheat your oven to 325°F.

- Line a baking sheet with parchment paper.

- In a large bowl, mix broad spectrum CBD oil,

flour, powdered milk, oatmeal, and peanut

butter.

- Add your egg with one cup of water; lightly

beat until the mixture is sticky.

• Move dough to a well-floured surface before

kneading into a ball.

• Push out the edges of your dough ball until you

create a flat, ½-inch thick disc.

• Cut treat-sized pieces from this disc and form

into balls.

• Place your balls on the baking sheet and brush

with egg wash.

• Bake for one hour or until treats are completely

hardened.

• Let sit for 15 minutes before serving your pups!

Cannabis Dog Treats Recipe

Ingredients:

• ½ Cup CBD Coconut Oil (See are Cannabis Oil

Recipe)

• 1 Cup Chicken Broth

• ¾ Cup Powdered Milk

• ½ Cup Peanut Butter

• 2 Large Eggs

• 4 Cups Whole Wheat Flour

Things you'll need

• Bowl

• Measuring cups

• Spatula

• Rolling pin or bottle of wine

• Cookie-cutter

• Sheet tray

• Cookie Sheet

Direction

1.) In a bowl mix pour in your Cannabis Oil,
Chicken Broth, Powdered Milk, Peanut butter, 2
large eggs and mix well.

2.) Add in the Whole wheat flour and again mix
until it forms into a dough.

3.) Knead the dough for a little while until
everything is well incorporated.

4.) On your kitchen table, dust a small area with whole wheat flour and place your Cannabis dog treat dough. Flatten it up and create an even surface using the rolling pin or you can use the side of a wine bottle.

5.) Cut the Dog Cannabis treats by using the cookie cutter. Place each one on the sheet tray covered with the cookie baking sheet.

6.) Bake the Cannabis Dog treats in the oven for 20-30 minutes at 275 degrees F or until the Cannabis Dog treats look dry and crunchy, similar to a cookie.

7.) Set aside to cool down and store in an airtight container for longer shelf life. Viola! You now have your homemade Cannabis Dog treats that

you can surprise your buddy with! Enjoy!

Peanut Butter and Pumpkin Pupcakes

Ingredients:

• 2 cups of oat flour

• 1 cup of rolled oats

• ½ cup of peanut butter

• ½ cup of pumpkin purée

• 1/3 cup of dehydrated apples

• ¼ cup of finely shredded coconut

• 2 eggs

- 1 tablespoon of Herbal Renewals Companion Hemp Extract or your favorite pet CBD oil

Directions:

- Combine all ingredients into a large bowl and knead to form dough.

- Preheat oven to 350°F. With a melon scooper scoop dough to form biscuits.

- Place biscuits o to a baking sheet and bake in oven for 30 minutes.

- Once time is up remove from oven and allow to cool.

Ingredients

• 1 cup pumpkin puree

• 1/2 cup unflavored Greek yogurt

• 1 teaspoon Herbal Renewals Companion Hemp

Extract or your favorite pet CBD oil

Directions:

• Mix the pumpkin puree, Greek yogurt, and CBD

oil together.

• Pour the mixture into silicone molds or an ice

cube tray.

• Freeze for at least two hours.

• Store in the freezer until ready to serve.

Sweet Potato Dog Treats

Ingredients:

- 2 medium sweet potatoes, cooked and cooled

- ½ cup coconut flour

- ½ cup coconut oil or bacon grease

- 1 egg

- 1 teaspoon Herbal Renewals Companion Hemp

Extract or your favorite pet CBD oil

- 1 to 2 tablespoons water

Directions:

- Preheat your oven to 350 degrees.

• Mix all of the ingredients together until well combined. Add extra coconut flour if necessary to achieve a consistency similar to Play-Doh.

• Form into balls about one inch in diameter. Flatten the balls with the palm of your hand.

• Place flattened balls onto a baking sheet lined with parchment paper.

• Bake for about 20 minutes. Remove and let cool before serving or storing.

No-Bake Coconut Dog Treats

Ingredients:

• 2½ cups rolled oats

• 1/3 cup coconut oil

• 3 tablespoons peanut butter

• 1 teaspoon Herbal Renewals Companion Hemp

Extract or your favorite pet CBD oil

• ½ cup shredded coconut

Directions:

• Mix together the coconut oil, peanut butter,

rolled oats, and CBD oil until combined (a food

processor is recommended, but you can do this

by hand).

• Scoop out bite-sized pieces with a spoon. Roll

the pieces into small balls.

• Place each ball into a bowl of shredded coconut, tossing and sprinkling until each ball is well-coated in coconut.

• Place the balls onto a flat tray or baking sheet lined with parchment paper. Refrigerate for about 30 minutes before you serve or store.

Frozen Peanut Butter Yogurt Treats

Ingredients:

• 1 cup peanut butter

• 32 ounces vanilla yogurt

• 1 teaspoon Herbal Renewals Companion Hemp Extract or your favorite pet CBD oil

Directions:

• Place the peanut butter in a microwave-safe bowl. Cover the bowl and microwave on high for 30 seconds. Stir the peanut butter. Repeat until the peanut butter is melted and easy to pour.

• Combine the yogurt and CBD oil into the peanut butter. Stir thoroughly to make sure the CBD gets mixed in properly.

• Pour the mixture into silicone molds or an ice cube tray. (Spray the ice cube tray with a non-stick spray first.)

• Leave the mold or tray in the freezer for about two hours or until the treats are fully frozen.

• You can increase or decrease the amount of CBD oil in each of these recipes depending on your dog's needs. Start low and slow if your dog hasn't used CBD before.

Sweet Potato and Yogurt CBD-Enriched Dog Treats

This is also a no-bake recipe that is super easy to do. The mashed sweet potato can be exchanged for mashed pumpkin. These delicious cold treats are perfect for the warm summer months!

Ingredients

• 1 cup sweet potato, cooked and mashed

• ½ cup plain yogurt

- 1 tbsp. coconut oil

- CBD oil

Direction

- Mix the yogurt with the sweet potato mash and coconut oil in a large bowl. Ensure its mixed thoroughly.

- Scoop the mixture into silicon molds or ice trays.

- Add CBD oil to each treat. If your dog needs one drop of CBD oil a day, add one drop to each treat.

- Put the trays or molds into the freezer for about three hours.

- Store in the freezer until ready to serve

CONCLUSION

With the huge popularity of CBD for use as a

natural supplement for both pets and people,

CBD has proved beneficial in natural healing and

treating inflammation and pain. CBD products

are the rage right now, but to get the best CBD

pet products, one needs to look for NASC –

approved.

www.ingramcontent.com/pod-product-compliance
Lightning Source LLC
Chambersburg PA
CBHW060911130726
48001CB00006B/2198